MANA-ZUCCA
kaleidoscope
six colorful piano solos

Edited by JOHN W. SCHAUM

FOREWORD

Mana-Zucca (pronounced MAH-na ZUCK-a) is the most prolific of American woman composers. Over 1100 of her compositions have been published, including music for the piano, violin, cello, flute and saxophone and for ballets and orchestras. She began as a child prodigy and went on to become a legend in her own time, a span that stretches from the time of Victor Herbert to today.

Biographical information, a photograph and the "Contents" appear on the next two pages.

SCHAUM PUBLICATIONS, INC.

2018 E. North Ave. Milwaukee, Wis. 53202

06 A42
FO-1

CONTENTS

BIOGRAPHICAL SKETCH

On December 25, 1894, Mana-Zucca was born to Jeannette Deneau and Samuel Shepard Zuccamana (she later reversed her surname and legalized "Mana-Zucca"). A child prodigy, she exhibited unusual talent in music at an early age. When only three years old, she was playing with a toy piano and happened to strike a melody in the key of G. But the black keys on the piano were only painted on and, unable to find the F# she needed, she burst into tears. A guest in her house recognized the problem and exclaimed, "That child has absolute pitch. She's unhappy because she can't find that sharp!" Lessons on a "real" piano soon followed.

Mana-Zucca went on to make her first public appearance at the age of four, performing standard works as well as improvising. At eight years of age she created a real sensation by playing a Beethoven Concerto with the New York Symphony Orchestra under the baton of Walter Damrosch.

In America Mana-Zucca studied the piano under Alexander Lambert and composition under Herman Spielter. Later she studied piano in Europe with Godowsky and Busoni, composition with Max Vogrich. At thirteen, she began a tour of the continent, concertizing in Russia, Germany, France, Holland and England.

She later married Irwin M. Cassel who also became her lyricist. When their son, Marwin S. Cassel, was born in 1925, Mana discontinued her composing for some time, but her husband encouraged her to start writing again. She took his advice and went on to find her place among the leading American composers. She has played her Piano Concerto with the Los Angeles Symphony Orchestra and the National Symphony Orchestra. Her orchestral compositions have been on the programs of the New York Philharmonic Orchestra, the Cincinnati Symphony Orchestra and the Russian Symphony Orchestra.

In 1974, Mana-Zucca was awarded a Doctor of Music degree by the University of Miami and recently received a scroll marking her 50th year as a member of the American Society of Composers, Authors and Publishers, ASCAP. She has been noted twice in the Congressional Record, which describes her as a "great American lady, a distinguished composer and pianist." As Senator Jacob K. Javits wrote to her later, "You are probably the only person who has appeared in the Record twice in one week in each house."

The compositions of Mana-Zucca are of unusual worth as to real interest and musical value. They show a rare creative ability and are always "melodic, musicianly and interesting." Since she is a superb pianist, it is only natural that her works for the piano are among her most notable.

Credit to the Miami Herald and the AMICA News Bulletin for biographical data.

Schaum Publications, Inc. is proud to present this collection of Mana-Zucca solos. At one of the Schaum workshops in Miami, Mana-Zucca was the honored guest. Also, on another occasion, Mr. Schaum was invited to her fabulous home where he visited with Mana and her husband Irwin. This was the showplace home known as Mazica Hall where many lavish receptions were held. It could accommodate an audience of 300 and provided the location of more than 500 concerts.

Although the days of Mazica Hall have passed, Mana-Zucca continues her music career. Living in Miami Beach, she still plays her piano daily and sponsors annual student recitals in her home each spring. In addition to her two grand pianos, her comfortable living room holds 200 other pianos - a collection of miniatures that includes the piano that started it all, a plywood model carved by her son many years ago.

SOUTHERN SERENADE

Mana-Zucca, Op. 296

Piu mosso
f agitato

rit.
Andante
molto cantabile
a tempo

WINTER WIND

Mana-Zucca, Op. 298

1. ↑ Tear off carefully, along perforation. ↑ 2. See "Directions" (on back side of this sheet) for complete information.

Order Form for Schaum Piano Teachers Guide

(Available ONLY to Piano or Organ Teachers)

Enclosed with this order form is a check or money order for $1.00, payable to Schaum Publications, Inc., for one copy of their catalog, the "Schaum Piano Teachers Guide." Cash sent only at risk of sender. See complete instructions and terms on other side of this sheet.

Accompanying this catalog shall be a Credit Coupon, redeemable within one year for $1.00 toward the purchase of any items listed in this catalog, when ordered directly from Schaum Publications, Inc.

Please PRINT clearly: ______________________________
NAME

____
STREET ADDRESS

____
CITY STATE ZIP CODE

To help us serve you better, please fill in answers to these questions:

How many PIANO students do you have? ________ (on the average)

Do you also teach ORGAN? ☐ YES ☐ NO

Do you use any of these PIANO METHODS:

"Making Music at the Piano"	☐ **Regularly**	☐ **Occasionally**	☐ **Never**
Schaum Course (A-B-C-D etc.)	☐ **Regularly**	☐ **Occasionally**	☐ **Never**
Thompson	☐ **Regularly**	☐ **Occasionally**	☐ **Never**
Glover	☐ **Regularly**	☐ **Occasionally**	☐ **Never**
Clark	☐ **Regularly**	☐ **Occasionally**	☐ **Never**
Pace	☐ **Regularly**	☐ **Occasionally**	☐ **Never**
Bastien	☐ **Regularly**	☐ **Occasionally**	☐ **Never**

Piano Teachers!

Obtain Your Own Copy of the Latest

SCHAUM PIANO TEACHERS GUIDE

(Complete Catalog of Schaum Publications, Inc.)

Cost: $1.00

—redeemable by the use of a coupon with an order sent to Schaum Publications, Inc., within one year (see details below).

INSTRUCTIONS:

1. Fill in your name & address clearly in the space provided on the order blank **(on other side of this sheet).**
2. Fill in the questionnaire section of the order form.
3. Make out check or money order for $1.00, payable to Schaum Publications, Inc. (Send cash at your own risk.)
4. Address an envelope to: SCHAUM PUBLICATIONS, INC.
   P.O. BOX 11946 MILWAUKEE, WI 53211
5. Include your own return-address on the envelope.
6. Enclose payment and completed order form in the envelope. Seal envelope and affix stamp for first class postage.

A CREDIT COUPON shall accompany your copy of the "Schaum Piano Teachers Guide." This coupon shall be redeemable for $1.00 toward the purchase of any items listed in the "Schaum Piano Teachers Guide," provided that the order is sent directly to Schaum Publications, Inc., and that the coupon be redeemed within one year from date of issue. Allow approximately 3 to 5 weeks for delivery of the "Teachers Guide." This catalog is available ONLY to Piano or Organ Teachers.

Piano Teachers!

Obtain Your Own Copy of the Latest

SCHAUM PIANO TEACHERS GUIDE

(Complete Catalog of Schaum Publications, Inc.)

Cost: $1.00

—redeemable by the use of a coupon with an order sent to Schaum Publications, Inc., within one year (see details below).

INSTRUCTIONS:

1. Fill in your name & address clearly in the space provided on the order blank (attached inside the back cover of this book).
2. Fill in the questionnaire section of the order form.
3. Make out check or money order for $1.00, payable to Schaum Publications, Inc. (Send cash at your own risk.)
4. Address an envelope to: SCHAUM PUBLICATIONS, INC.
   P.O. BOX 11946 MILWAUKEE, WI 53211
5. Include your own return-address on the envelope.
6. Enclose payment and completed order form in the envelope. Seal envelope and affix stamp for first class postage.

A CREDIT COUPON shall accompany your copy of the "Schaum Piano Teachers Guide." This coupon shall be redeemable for $1.00 toward the purchase of any items listed in the "Schaum Piano Teachers Guide," provided that the order is sent directly to Schaum Publications, Inc., and that the coupon be redeemed within one year from date of issue. Allow approximately 3 to 5 weeks for delivery of the "Teachers Guide." This catalog is available ONLY to Piano or Organ Teachers.

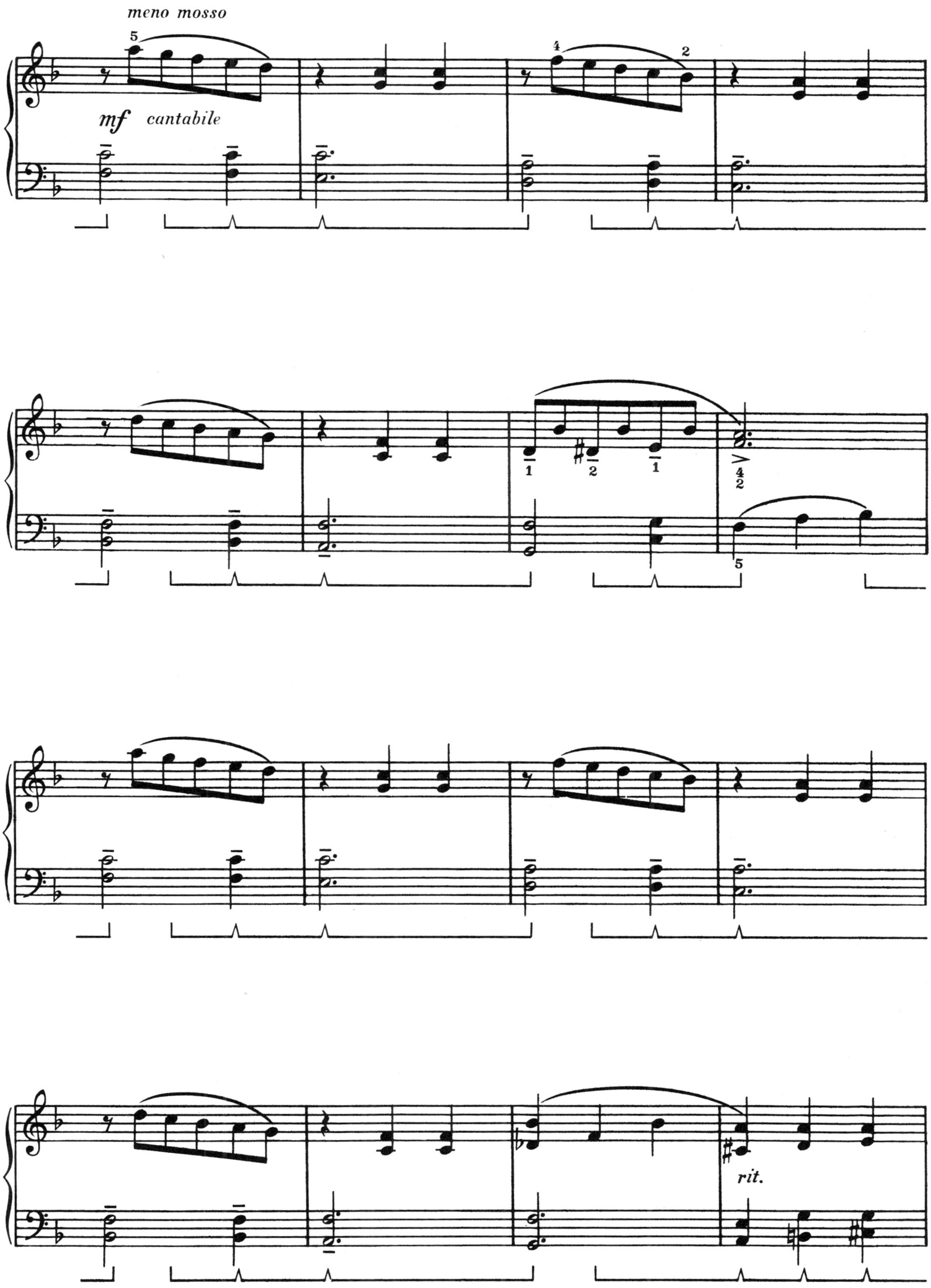
meno mosso
mf cantabile
rit.

mf
f
brillante
ff
fz

RUNNING BROOK

Mana-Zucca, Op. 302, No. 1

mf
ten.
rit.
a tempo
ten.
ten.
rit.

f a tempo
p
dim.
pp
f

DANCING LEAVES

Mana-Zucca, Op. 302, No. 2

Giocoso

One of the inconsistencies of printed music is the flexibility in performing this rhythm pattern . At times the composer means it to be played this way as for example in Nevin's "Narcissus". Many composers prefer to write the triplet rhythm this way because visually the individual beat or or count is more unified and the notes are less scattered. In "Dancing Leaves", it would obviously be typographically very confusing to use the triplet symbol.	From a performing standpoint, each composition where this pattern appears, is to be judged individually. When it occurs in combination with triplets as in "Dancing Leaves," it should be played in triplet rhythm .

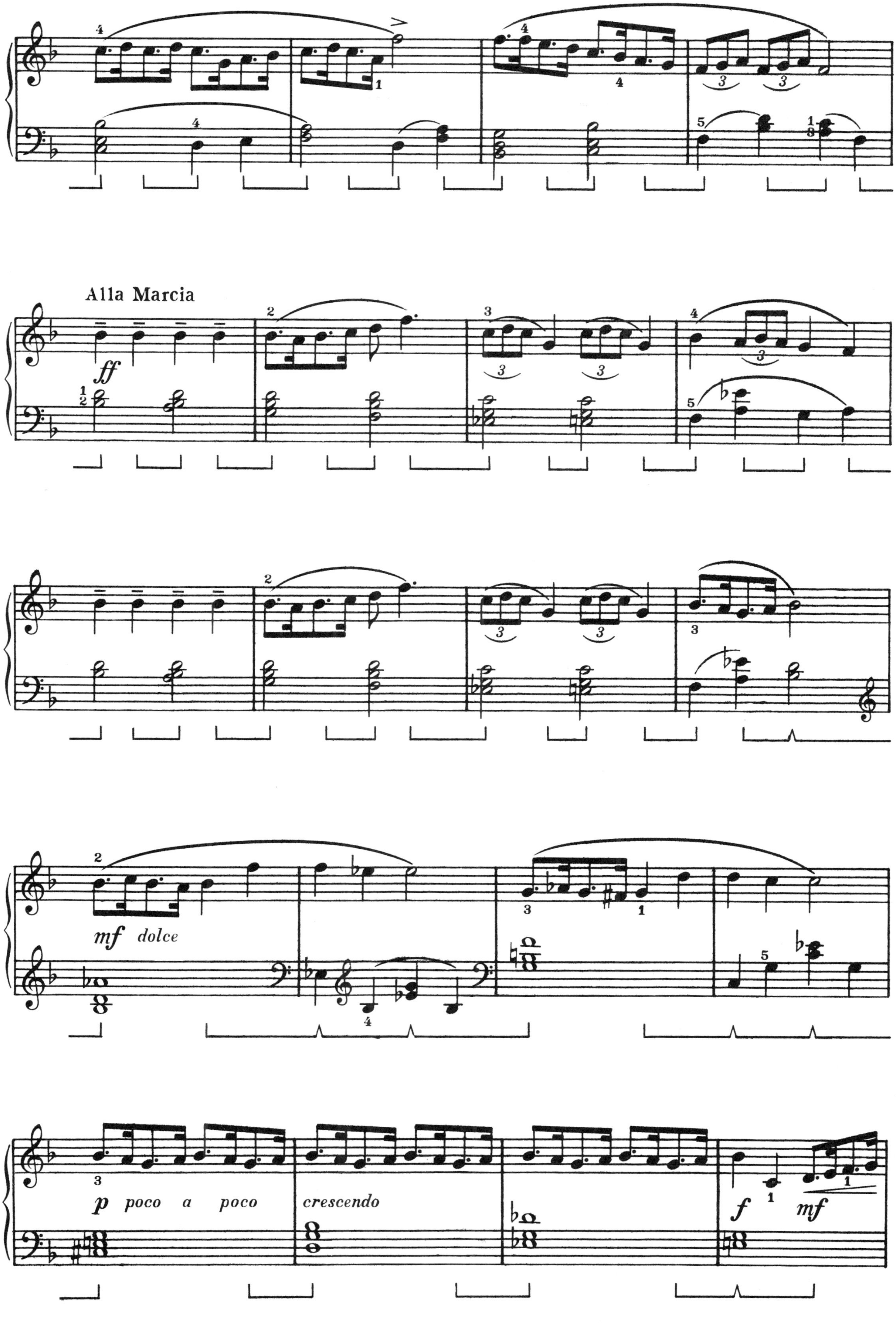
Alla Marcia
ff
mf dolce
p poco a poco
crescendo
f
mf

Giocoso

BIRDS IN FLIGHT

Mana-Zucca, Op. 302, No. 3

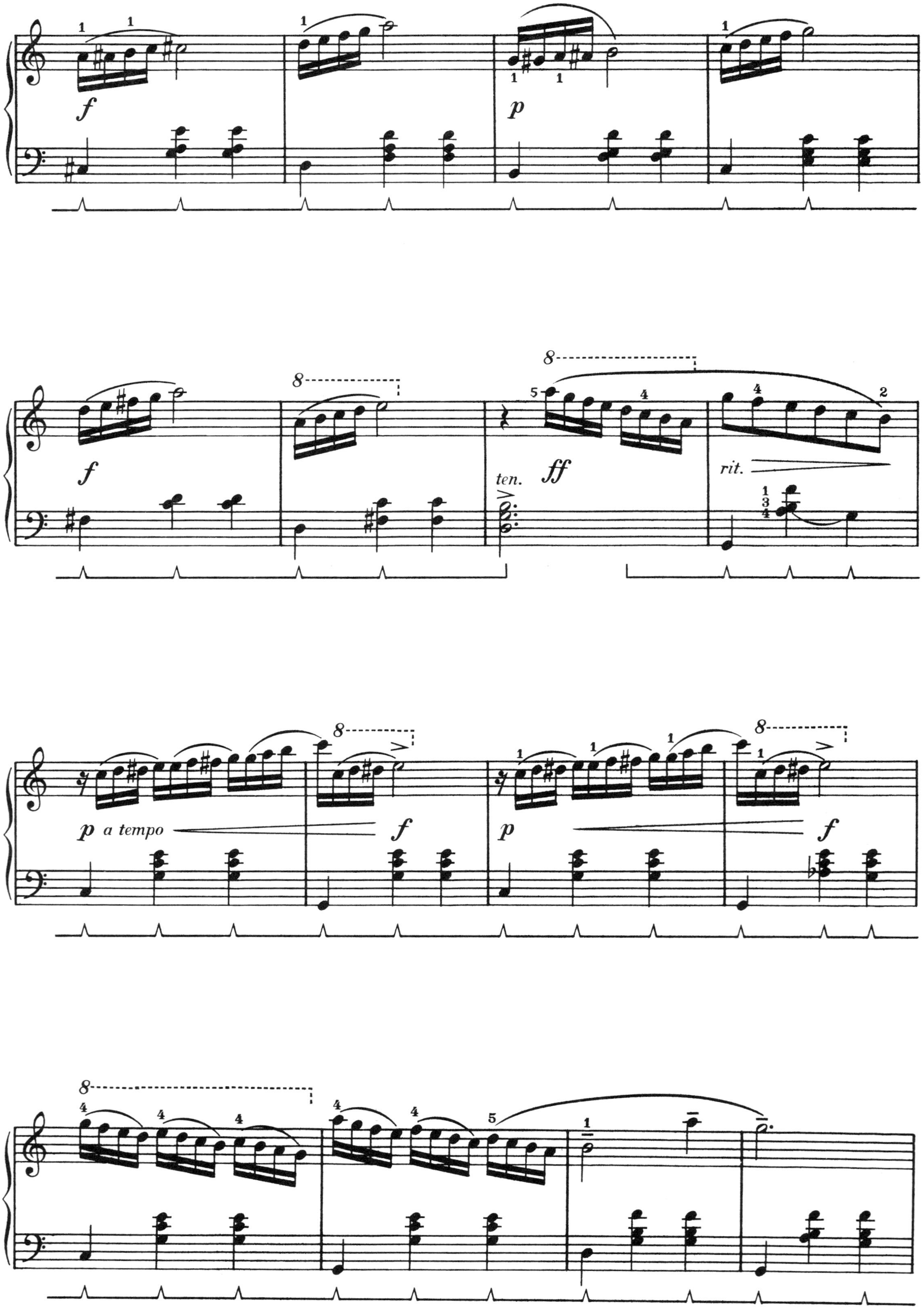
f
p
f
ten.
ff
rit.
p a tempo
f
p
f

ten.
cresc.

SUMMER SONATINA

Mana-Zucca, Op. 297

dolce
Con brio

Andante cantabile

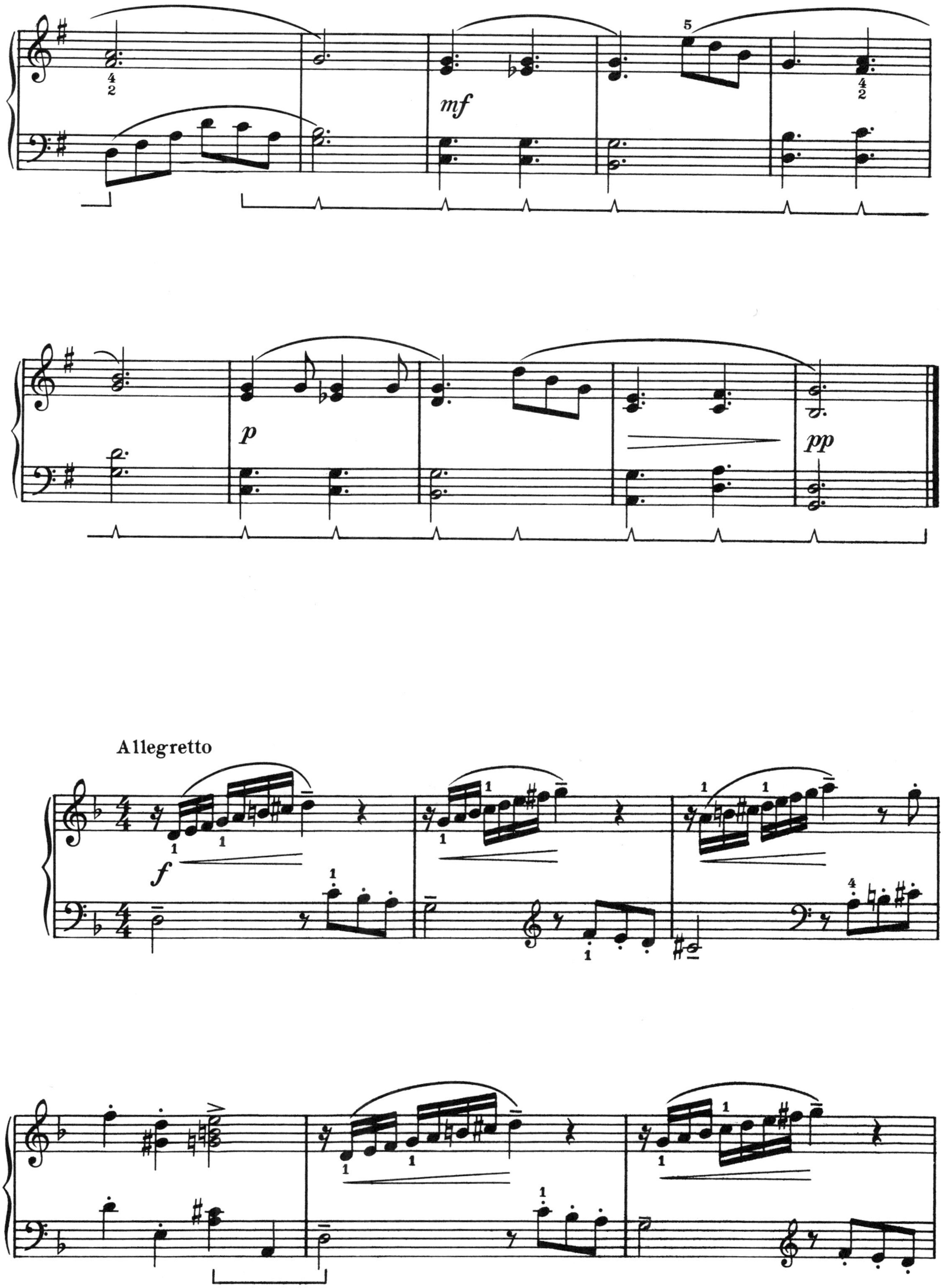
Allegretto

mf
f
p
mf
f
rit.

Schaum Sheet Music

This is a partial list — Showing Grade 2 thru Grade 4½ Titles

GRADE 2 – (C)

Beach Ball Boogie . . . *John W. Schaum*
Candy Man . . . *Bricusse & Newley*
Country Rock . . . *John Paul Jones*
Dixie . . . *Daniel D. Emmett*
Fascination Waltz . . . *F. D. Marchetti*
Give My Regards to Broadway . . . *Geo. M. Cohan*
Harmony . . . *Kaplan & Simon*
Hava Nagila . . . *Israeli Folk Dance*
I'm An Old Cowhand . . . *Johnny Mercer*
In the Mood . . . *Joe Garland*
Joy Prelude . . . *J. S. Bach*
Let It Snow! Let It Snow! Let It Snow! . . . *Jule Styne*
Lift Ev'ry Voice and Sing . . . *J. Rosamond Johnson*
Matchmaker . . . *Jerry Bock*
National Emblem March . . . *E. E. Bagley*
Only You . . . *Buck Ram & Ande Rand*
Pollution Solution . . . *John W. Schaum*
Red Sails in the Sunset . . . *Hugh Williams*
Road Runner . . . *John W. Schaum*
Send In the Clowns . . . *Stephen Sondheim*
Side by Side . . . *Harry Woods*
Sing, Robin Sing . . . *Geo. L. Spaulding*
Skate Board . . . *Wesley Schaum*
Ski Slope . . . *Phyllis Warfel*
Sleepy Lagoon . . . *Eric Coates*
South of the Border . . . *Kennedy & Carr*
Star-Spangled Banner . . . *Commemorative Edition*
Symphony No. 40 (First Theme) . . . *W. A. Mozart*
Texas Mother's Lullaby . . . *May Foreman Carr*
With These Hands . . . *Abner Silver*
Yankee Doodle Dandy . . . *Geo. M. Cohan*
You're a Grand Old Flag . . . *Geo. M. Cohan*

GRADE 2½ – (D)

Beethoven's Fifth Symphony . . . *1st Mvt. Theme*
Birthday Bouquet (Piano SOLO) . . . *(Theme & Variations)*
Caravan . . . *Rachel Beatty Kahl*
Consider Yourself . . . *Lionel Bart*
Entertainer (Piano SOLO) . . . *Scott Joplin*
Fiddler on the Roof . . . *Jerry Bock*
Funeral March of a Marionette . . . *Gounod*
Fur Elise . . . *Beethoven*
Guantanamera . . . *Latin American Folk Song*
I Believe . . . *Drake, Graham, Shirl & Stillman*
Marshmallow World . . . *Peter DeRose*
Melody in F . . . *Anton Rubinstein*
Minuet Medley . . . *Bach*

GRADE 2½ – (continued)

Moment Musical . . . *Schubert*
Mountain Majesty . . . *Willa Waid Newman*
On the Sunny Side of the Street . . . *Jimmy McHugh*
Santa's On His Way . . . *John W. Schaum*
Second Hand Rose . . . *James F. Hanley*
Shark Hunt . . . *Edward J. Plank*
Sonata in C . . . *Mozart*
Turkish March . . . *Mozart*
Where Is Love? (from "Oliver") . . . *Lionel Bart*
Where the River Shannon Flows . . . *Russell*
Yankee Doodle . . . *(Theme & Variations)*

GRADE 3 – (E)

Avalanche *(original form)* . . . *Stephen Heller*
Blue Danube . . . *Johann Strauss, Jr.*
Candy Cane Lane . . . *Agnes D. Kastler*
Corsage Waltz . . . *John W. Schaum*
Cotton Pickin' Boogie . . . *Wm. H. Myddleton*
Danse Macabre . . . *Saint-Saens*
Etude in E Major . . . *Chopin*
Hallelujah Chorus . . . *Handel*
Hawaiian Nocturne . . . *Ladonna Weston*
Neapolitan Serenade . . . *Enrico Toselli*
On Wings of Fantasy . . . *Bea Lewis*
Oriental Nocturne . . . *Alexander Borodin*
Rustle of Spring . . . *Sinding*
Valse Triste . . . *Sibelius*

GRADE 4 – (F)

Ave Maria . . . *Schubert*
Christmas Fantasy . . . *Moore-Schaum*
Clair de Lune . . . *Debussy*
Forgotten Waltz . . . *Liszt*
Greensleeves . . . *Cameo Transcription*
Jingle Bells Jubilee . . . *Concert Transcription*
Journey To Bethlehem . . . *Cecelia D. Williams*
Kiss Me Again . . . *Victor Herbert*
La Danza . . . *Rossini*
Lento . . . *Cyril Scott*
March of the Toys . . . *Victor Herbert*
Solfeggietto *(original form)* . . . *C.P.E. Bach*
Toyland . . . *Victor Herbert*
Whistler and his Dog . . . *Arthur Pryor*

GRADE 4½ – (G)

After Theater Tango . . . *Zez Confrey*
Humoresque . . . *Dvorak—Concert Transcription*
Lotus Land . . . *Cyril Scott*
Mexican Hat Dance . . . *Concert Transcription*
Symphonic Rhapsody . . . *Franck*

PIANO DUETS – (1 Piano, 4 Hands)

Birthday Bouquet *(Theme & Variations)* . . . (2½)
Entertainer *(Scott Joplin)* . . . *(2½)*
Parade of the Toy Soldiers *(Jessel)* . . . *(1)*

Schaum Publications, Inc., Milwaukee, Wis. 53202